I WOULD DEFINE THE SUN

I WOULD DEFINE THE SUN

poems

STEPHANIE NIU

FOREWORD BY
MAJOR JACKSON

VANDERBILT UNIVERSITY PRESS
Nashville, Tennessee

Copyright 2025 by Stephanie Niu
Published by Vanderbilt University Press.
All rights reserved.
First printing 2025

Library of Congress Cataloging-in-Publication Data
Names: Niu, Stephanie, 1997- author.
Title: I would define the sun : poems / Stephanie Niu.
Description: Nashville, Tennessee : Vanderbilt University Press, 2025. |
Series: VU literary prize ; vol 5
Identifiers: LCCN 2024053269 (print) | LCCN 2024053270 (ebook) | ISBN
9780826507716 (paperback) | ISBN 9780826507723 (epub) | ISBN
9780826507730 (pdf)
Subjects: LCGFT: Poetry.
Classification: LCC PS3614.I88 I33 2025 (print) | LCC PS3614.I88 (ebook)
| DDC 811/.6--dc23/eng/20241118
LC record available at https://lccn.loc.gov/2024053269
LC ebook record available at https://lccn.loc.gov/2024053270
This publication was made possible with the support of the McEntire Literary
Prize Endowment and Vanderbilt University's Office of the Chancellor.

Established in 2024, the Vanderbilt University Literary Prize
is awarded annually to the sole author of a full-length collection
of poetry that demonstrates great poignancy combined
with rigor in form, language, and artistic vision.

GENERAL EDITOR: Major Jackson
JURISTS: Victoria Chang, Dana Levin, and Gregory Pardlo

FRONT COVER IMAGE: Photo by Roman Melnychuk via Unsplash

For my family, always
And for my teachers

Contents

    Foreword by Major Jackson   xi
    If Words Cost Nothing   1

I   After Eden   5
    The World's Heart   6
    Learning Money in Reverse   7
    Information Worker at the End of the World   8
    What do coral even get stressed about?   9
    My Mother Says Water Dreams Are Auspicious   10
    I Crossed the Sea Boardwalk   11

II   Christmas Island   15
    Garbage Boogie   16
    Midden / Appetite   18
    Sonnet of Tropical Excess   20
    Keeping House   21
    Hummingbirds   22
    Hilton Head   23
    By These Things We Live   24

III   Endeavour   27
    Abecedarian for Pinyin   29
    Study in Blue   31
    兰   32
    While Peering in the Mirror   33

One Blue Sound 34
Missing You 35
青 36
Hymn 37
The Road from the Mountains 38

IV Before Desire 41
Lake Lanier 42
The Ocean in Miniature 44
Leaving Lisbon 45
Phenomenology Study / Elegy for Island Love 46
Recurring Dream of Escape 47
He Sleeps 48
She Has Dreamt Again of Water 49
Returning to the Village 50
I Met My Loneliness 51
I Drive as My Family Sleeps 52

V 老家 55
The Question 56
The Magic of Eating Garbage 57
Bracing Myself Against Sea Wind Along the Coast You Call Home 58
Migration 59
Today Is 61
Motherhood in the Climate Crisis 62
Sea Swim 63

CODA 大连 / Dalian 67

Notes 69
Acknowledgments 75

I thought
that pain meant
I was not loved.
It meant I loved.

—LOUISE GLÜCK,
"FIRST MEMORY"

Foreword

Major Jackson

Reading some poets' poems you get the sense that they frequently stand on a bluff high above the ocean, like Caspar David Friedrich's *Wanderer Above the Sea of Fog*, looking out at the horizon, oblivious to the affairs of human beings behind them. Other books of poetry read like aestheticized history lessons or dispatches from the land of unkindness; far too many set out to argue cultural relevance or render legible codes of survival. Occasionally, one encounters a voice so attuned to the groundswell of their being that their poems arrive like luxuriant explorations of language and feeling. Such is the work of Stephanie Niu and her debut collection of poetry *I Would Define the Sun*. Consider, for example, these passages from her opening poems:

> I would stretch and remember species
> of phytoplankton older than desire.
>
> I would age like plankton. I would desire
> you outside of a body, outside time.
>
> In time, you stand outside with a body.
> I will love you with nothing but words.
>
> —"IF WORDS COST NOTHING"

> When I woke, blood fell out of me.
> When I broke the heart of my first
>
> and best love, I thought I was good
> at being alone. I thought good
>
> people were something to protect
> from myself. I left. I kept leaving
>
> —"AFTER EDEN"

Some plankton are as old as two hundred million years. To claim desire that lasts as long might sound like an exercise in hyperbole, but if nothing else, we know the speaker feels passionately; lucky is the person who is the object of her attention. It is refreshing how so much unguarded emotion is claimed in *I Would Define the Sun* without the least bit of embarrassment or irony.

Such effusive, full-throated lines defy contemporary treatises on poetry and stand outside social orthodoxies; Niu dares originality by courting sincerity. The geography of the heart mapped onto marine life, or masked behind an iconic biblical figure, startles us for its explicit declarations that afford her an unabashed voice. These poems are not bound by constraint. They do not shy away from the beauty and messiness of living. They risk feeling as they aim for the highest reaches of the art.

For most of this collection, Niu maintains an exalted pitch of expressiveness that reinforces the believability of her speakers, which is no small act for it might be the most urgent imperative of poetry today, that is, to convince a reader that the epiphanies found here are bred from a human life and not the product of large language models and manipulation of data points. Yet Niu counterbalances and renders us aware of the artifice of making; there's a reflexive quality throughout the book that endures for how it completes her intelligence. "I will love you with nothing but words," she writes. In another poem she says, "I cannot achieve incomprehensibility without singing."

Niu's singing maps her virtuosity. Under the towering shadow of poetic tradition, especially its fruitful excesses of experimentation, poets must achieve a set of benchmarks.

They must mark their originality by orienting us back to our luminous fates as blood and flesh beings who are haunted by time. In so doing, they provide pathways to understanding our seemingly impenetrable journeys on earth. Niu sets about this by, among other approaches, plunging headlong into a lyric presence that mourns the gradual degradation of our planet ("the earth is more burned out than my coworkers"), that celebrates nature and its creatures ("The ocean is a wedding waiting room. . . . Here every dream is still possible"), that thinks through the large global crises but not at the expense of documenting her personal calamities ("My greatest sin must be that I still dream / of disappearing").

The speaker in her poems does not absolve herself, nor stand on high moral ground. She writes, "Is it bad that in the crash / of trash down the chute I hear / music?" The internal rhyme and soft rustling of the "sh" enacts a redemptive sound.

Niu also articulates the challenge of cultural representation and the urgency of locating her freedom. In "Recurring Dream of Escape," a speaker states,

> I swim
> in the sea. I am, for once,
> nothing, smaller than nothing,
> beholden to no one, friendless,
> unmeasured, unwitnessed,
> and in this way finally free.

In a racialized body, the wish to be subsumed by the ocean is the equivalent of writing into the true sources of one's experiences, so that what emerges is an authenticating work that distills the actual life *behind* these poems into a mythic level of seeing. This must be why dreams are such a motif in this collection, for it is in dreams that the debris of our existence gives way to latent desires and fears embodied in fragmented and surreal images. One of my favorites in the book, "My Mother Says Water Dreams Are Auspicious," has the speaker celebrating the migration of animals from her mother's dream into her own. In another, a sister seeds a myth that sends the speaker on an imagined journey to a village of dead bodies at the bottom of a lake. The whimsy of Niu's imagination freights her poems with all manner of intrigue.

Furthermore, the poet must also make known that their poems emerge from more than a single source of inspiration, which, in the highly trafficked world of poetry publishing and the ongoing competition for our empathy and attention, causes single-subject project books to frequently collide into their own importance. Niu has given a form to her intellectual and emotional restlessness. In addition to dwindling ecologies and cultural identities, she is compelled by class issues, Christmas Island, and the vicissitudes of love, both how we soar and why we flee.

Yet, no matter her subject, formal elements amplify these themes with remarkable painterly care. Her approach is one of a watercolorist. And though her mind buzzes with prodigious activity, she ruminates and does not obsess. Within sight are, for example, the color blue, human appetites and waste, moments of familial bonding, and existential loneliness.

> I wonder if we know how to be with each other
> without labor. Even this journey north to clear out
> an old warehouse by ourselves, the five of us
> refusing to hire help, proves just how far we'll travel
> for a meal together.

One of the surprises of the book is the impressive use of poetic forms including sestina, sonnet, and an abecedarian. Niu is masterful for how she gently renders and places them throughout the book. Poetic form prevents her work from suffering an insularity or her lyric meditations from remaining proximate to their own thinking. She finds ways of transforming the ordinary into the mysterious.

One can visualize, without much effort, "a halo around a fading tattoo" and "flammable trees that form a cathedral." Instead of overly abstracting the real world, she collaborates with it; one senses her abundant joy in conjuring images that take us back to the substance of her desire.

Finally, the poet must capture the dignity and sanctity of the human, to faithfully reproduce the inner life of a woman living in the twenty-first century. We are bound on all sides by forces that work to obscure the sacredness of humanity. Poetry has a way of pushing back against the policies, technologies, and ideologies that would demean and reduce our lives. Niu is invested in poetry that deepens our understanding of how we relate as beings. ("We begin with the end but do not end there.") It takes courage and discipline to write clearly and to cultivate trust in a reader through the intimate act of naming. In so doing, the author gifts us ways to be *and* feel, then translates and transforms her thoughts and observations into a singularly heard sound. It is clear to me that Stephanie Niu's *I Would Define the Sun* is that wonderful of a book. She exercises an expanse of seeing fitting for the complexity of our world.

If Words Cost Nothing

If words cost nothing, I would use them
to build a bridge and cross into the sea.

    I would build the sea and bridge across
    the seven named zones defined by sun.

I would have seven names. I would define the sun.
At night, I would collect sentences with a net,

    let night collect into a sentence
    stretching across species and memory.

I would stretch and remember species
of phytoplankton older than desire.

    I would age like plankton. I would desire
    you outside of a body, outside time.

In time, you stand outside with a body.
I will love you with nothing but words.

After Eden

When I woke, blood fell out of me.
When I broke the heart of my first

and best love, I thought I was good
at being alone. I thought good

people were something to protect
from myself. I left. I kept leaving

for years, to an island surrounded
by days of water. I took

leaving literally. I shook
unripe papayas from papery trees

long before I learned how to eat them.
I left the island. I returned.

I failed to catch fish.
I dreamt of my love making

cynical quips in an abandoned theater.
I abandoned the island to see him.

He was the same. I was different,
sorrier. I said I was sorry. He said

I don't remember exactly how it ended.
He had nothing to forgive me for. I left

for the island. I let the jungle foliage
lace my calves with cuts. I slept poorly.

I love him. I cannot stop
writing this poem.

The World's Heart

is left of where I think
to look: not the child crying
in the carriage but the stuffed
cat he holds—gray fur, white socks,
lighter than a nickel. Not my lover in the park
confessing the distance he feels
but blown bubbles climbing the sky
behind him like krill.

When my mother let herself bleed
onto gas station concrete
somewhere west of Arizona, heat
from the hills blurred her spilled red
onto my hands. If I sliced the world open
just below the gills, I'd find another fish
inside, scarlet and going still.

Learning Money in Reverse

My mother can still afford to retire.
She withdraws her offer on the foreclosed house.

My drunken signature vanishes from a receipt.
Friends dodge disappearing plates of sushi.

Boxes of takeout repackage themselves,
I un-sign my first lease, I go home.

My parents remarry. I have not yet chosen
the school that will cost their life savings.

I close and seal the scholarship rejections.
My first paystub folds back into thirds.

My forehead unkisses the floor and I pass
the red envelope back to my mother.

We move into a smaller, more crowded house,
where I fry sesame seeds with 姥姥, and the HOA

reprimands us for growing winter melon on the porch.
I pedal backwards on my sister's bike. I hand back

her worn clothes. We put coins from our palms
back into our father's coat, having told him *good job*

because we think this is what he earns in a day,
and it's enough. He's about to come home.

Information Worker at the End of the World

When the ship to Mars has already departed,
and my wealthiest friends have plots in New Zealand
for their children, or have no children, what box
do I put my treasure in? I have one waterproof bag
that clips at the top. Every month, money drips
into my retirement account. *You think the world
will still be around when you're sixty-five?* I don't know
what it means to survive. I've learned all I can
about the Svalbard seed vault. I used to spend time
on the names of birds until the warblers disappeared.
The earth is more burned out than my coworkers.
The mantle is deathly dry. My doctor tells me
I ought to moisturize. Weekly, my milk expires.
I panic when I flip to a new month on my free
Audubon calendar. There is too much time
and not enough of it. I'm a bad steward caught
red-eyed. I board flights, order takeout high,
forget to recycle. Some days I wake and resolve
to arm myself for a righteous fight. I will make
coffee grounds into face scrub, eat kombucha
bacteria raw! Other days I wake already late
to my first meeting, say *hello* brightly
though the laptop screen is all my gunked-up
eyes can see. A blue glow sized to a day, an hour,
an act of speech. Everything else beyond me.

What do coral even get stressed about?

Current events / As in, the election / US-Russia sanctions / Coral takes one look / at the police officer on trial and bleaches / It's a wonder coral can live / when black men are dying / through state-sanctioned violence / Coral gets overwhelmed / by misinformation / Coral forgets / all its passwords / The feed replacing coral's / food source is toxic / Coral goes mindless / Coral gets stuck refreshing / Too many cycles for coral / to keep up with / News cycle / Water cycle / Nitrogen to filter / spilled industrial garbage / Coral cannot afford health insurance / Coral becomes insomniac / Coral sleeps poorly / when blanketed by volcanic ash

My Mother Says Water Dreams Are Auspicious

the night after I dream of rising side-by-side with a whale shark. We begin in water, move indoors. We float past the couch of my childhood living room. Swimming approximates flight, as in life. That same night, my mother dreamed of slaying a snake, cutting its long body like a carrot. I feel her pride at the way lucky animals migrate from her sleep to mine. The night before her second miscarriage, she dreamed of a body tucked into a closet. When she opened the door, the body's head rolled out. When she opened her eyes, the body's head was already exiting her. As in life, images approximate meaning. We begin in water, float through childhood. At times we cleave to live.

I Crossed the Sea Boardwalk

tentatively as if entering
back into a dream. Faulty beams
were marked with orange cones.
I stepped lightly. My blue dress blew
in the wind, long and impractical.
In practice, I had been here before.
I had practiced returning for years
in my mind. When I reached the clearing,
I was devastated to find nothing
had changed. The ice plants
sat green, wet, chalky with salt.
Limestone jagged toward the horizon.
The blue-billed seabirds regarded me
with warranted suspicion.

If the dream is dreamlike as real life,
I reasoned, then nothing can be real.
Yet I sat in a patch of matted grass seasoned
with salt I could feel. The mystery of eels
is that we don't know exactly how they breed.
Aristotle thought they come from nothing.
The miracle is that there is any other way
to arrive. I am saying I stepped off
the same boardwalk twice. Behind me,
a plane left the island carrying someone I love.
Ice plants carry entire seasons of water
in their leaves. Drunk from the air.
Come from nothing. I came from nothing
and when I returned, it was still there.

II

Christmas Island

Here, apples are more expensive than meat.
Everything comes by plane biweekly—ice-crusted
freezers await mummified lettuce heads in tropical heat.
I chop tinned Spam for protein. I am always hungry.
My host brings home fish he caught
the day before: white wahoo, firm chunks
almost translucent. These fish I swam with
this morning, their long bodies glinting like blades.

I slice into the meat. I will eat this seared,
with soy sauce and juice from the neighbor's
calamansi tree. I imagine the chase,
the long body twisting in evening light.
The clear fins trembling in a truck bed.
I taste the fish. I wish for more.

Garbage Boogie

Is it bad that in the crash
of trash down the chute I hear
music? The sound of hollow boxes
and old bottles of booze
lulls me, confused, into its groove:
I have trash guilt. I'm culpable.
Though I compost, sort my
recyclables. I know that no
amount of used glass
can amount to real absolution.
A friend suggests we throw it
into space as the solution. My date's dad
is a psycho recycler, I remember
as I pass a strangely fragrant can.
He sorts everything, the chopsticks
and their wrapper separately bagged.
We can't all be like him. The system
can't need us to be superhuman.
Of course I toss takeout containers
without rinsing the grease first.
What am I if not a glutton
for convenience? Waste is easy
as moldy tomatoes tossed in the bin.
I discard what I can't carry.
Cheap furniture. Responsibility.

The ambitious bag of bacteria
for kombucha never brewed,
still fizzing miraculously.
I empty myself gladly. Trash knows.
It barrels into a bulge, shows off
the ways we still overflow
with hunger, so much hunger
with nowhere to go.

Midden / Appetite

My mother calls herself our trash heap.
She eats what we won't, grows plump
on our leftover eggs, bread crusts,
the bitter-hearted lotus seeds we cannot stomach.
We have small appetites. Waiting for us means eating,
cutting slice after slice of pumpkin bread
until all the bowls are clean.
No one wants to be garbage, she says,
but look what I do for you.

In archaeology a trash heap is called a *midden*.
It means you've struck gold. What better map
to the way people lived than the things they discarded:
oysters shells, chicken bones, bits of green glass,
pickle forks, shoe leather miraculously intact.
The trash tells what they used, what they ate,
what they could not afford to throw away.
No buttons. No jewelry. In a California midden
where Chinese orchard workers lived
they found a single bottle for baby formula,
cracked. The glass so old it flakes,
iridescent, dragonfly wings catching light.

My mother does not like the way she looks.
In the dressing room she pinches the flesh
around her face. *If someone loved me more,
maybe I wouldn't gain weight.*

When a whale dies and sinks to the sea floor,
a world emerges to devour it. Hagfish come first,
faceless mouths chewing at the skin.
Then larger fish, sharks even, eyes
rolling as they tear into flesh.
A fallen whale sustains this ecosystem for years.
Even its skeleton becomes a home.

My mother talks of death often—her knees hurt,
she cannot sleep, her eyes worsen each day.
Put my body in the earth, she says,
breaking sunflower seeds after dinner.
I do not want to become food.

Sonnet of Tropical Excess

Woke and vacuumed. Took damp clothes
off the line for the coming storm. Living
with the shore at your door is constant
war. No use wiping salt off the counter:
there's more. Sand in every filter. All my books
are warped. My hair sticks to itself every morning.

I dreamed of coming back here for five years.
I arrived and remembered the rainy season:
how it renders beaches mean and crushing.
Can our selves across time warn? I know mine can
lure—younger, I desired this island so strongly
I carved a path that stayed clear for years.
Even earlier, islandless, I was in love.
I still don't know what I wanted more of.

Keeping House

Windfall pears sleep like rocks
at the base of a tree. The baseboard
needs sealing before the next heavy rain
heaves a garden snake into the kitchen.

So unlikely, the small body
glistening next to the cut
tennis balls fitted over chair feet.
Its skin liquid and textureless
as the tadpole we caught from the pond
and kept in a tank in the living room
for two years, where it never became a frog.
After, we poured the water and its body
into the backyard. The living loom
over the other living. In the dream
where I flew, I plucked helicopters
from the air as if they had tails
and not rudders. In real life, I hold
a squirming tadpole still. The attic trap snaps
behind the thin bloom of a squirrel. I do not have

the words to keep everything alive. My mother
stands over the snake and raises her arms.

Hummingbirds

It happens after dinner. It happens in the field
near the dry creek bed where old clothes gather

by crushed boxes of soap and candy wrappers.
Here, with the fading light and your bad eyes,

robins congregate, their rusty breasts all you can make
out against the grass. A bee sniffs for the remains

of some sweet dinner in your hair. The day
angles itself toward darkness. You hear

some low machine-hum, think of the trucks
that transferred a hundred sick prisoners

into the cells of the well. Five men died today.
That low-sky chopper sound means danger

as surely as smoke means flame, though you are miles
from the fire. There is so much you cannot contain—

the sick, the dead, the acres lost—that when you lean back
and see hummingbirds, their small beating wings, their neat

gleaming bodies nearly armored, you cannot help smiling
at how cruel they are, so sleek in their beautiful knowing,

and in spite of yourself you remember what else
is still there when you look up, squinting:

pines, stars, planets—things that never seem to leave
the sky but stare back, bright beyond understanding.

Hilton Head

As if this beach is not the place
of their earliest unraveling, each balanced
on a bike, my pregnant mother reluctant,
trusting her doomsayer sense until
it happens again, she is right, she is falling
in a tangle of toothed gears and sand, her knee
suddenly gushing, my father watching
her enormous belly press down. The dead
jellyfish here wash up so cleanly
compared to other kinds of death,
no blood, just clear bodies deflating
in a neat row. Now when we bike
she is collected, eyeing the tide line,
pointing out the parts of jellies
that are good to eat. The clear bell
to rinse in cold water. The froth
of tentacles to slice off clean. Now
who will help me gather the beautiful meat?

By These Things We Live

As if the universe would not be much without us
to comprehend it back. We who praise

anything with hemispheres, a waist. Our soft, halved
brains. Our own split globe. So close to self

recognition it nearly frays. Bach's last piece,
unfinished, spells his name in the notes.

He got so close it killed him. Or, strangely,
so we hope. We return to foundations.

The other golden record sounds. We hope
they are enough, drive home from work.

We go for walks. The marsh grass takes in salt
until its round tips redden and drop off.

Away in space, they play our best and proudest sounds:
rain, earthquakes, the bark of wild dogs.

III

Endeavour

In the International Space Station, a sequined
  dinosaur rotates, midair.

One astronaut's son calls out "I love you Mommy!"
  before his mother enters the spacecraft.

So far, we've spent one billion dollars per person sent
  up.

"We" here means the United States.

My mother studied to be an astronaut in another
  country, laughs now at how far her life is
  from rockets.

The first years in Huntsville, she drove hours across
  the state border with my father to buy soy sauce.

Like deer, they followed salt away from Rocket City.

I imagine the universe where my mother jokes with
  mission control – "先蹦一蹦,在看!"

Her words naturally contain the moon (月), the
  object of her gaze (目).

The words we use have what we need within them.

In orbit, the astronauts named their rocket
  Endeavour.

My mother asked for what she wanted in her
  passwords, the typed stars recording without
  revealing her desires.

When the rocket's four parachutes finally filled, we began to breathe again.

We begin with the end but do not end there.

Once the rocket contacted water, the filled bells unfurled like some god's dropped napkin.

✳ ✳ ✳ ✳ ✳ ✳ ✳ ✳ ✳ ✳ ✳ ✳ = godblessmeaboy

What isn't inevitable: how we cheer when they return to earth.

How deer return to the same salted woods.

How prayer can be the size of a word:

Dear God, bless our end.

Dear end, devour me a boy.

Dear boy, an end can mean our blessed good – 看!

Abecedarian for Pinyin

Ah is the first and easiest sound for a child to make,
Over the doctor's popsicle-stick probe or at the kitchen
  table,
Entreaty for another warm spoonful. *Ah* is the first
  spell we learn to sound out,
Invitation miraculously saying *Here is a want I trust
  you to
Understand and fill.* We practiced the other vowels like
  songs, even
Ü which sounds like the word for *fish*. The consonants,
  too, shone
Bright on their poster, *de* a horse's hoof, *te* an umbrella
  handle, letters
Placed to form a chant, swelling into each other and
  crackling in our
Mouths. When a new student from China named John
  joined my
Fifth grade class, I was quickly appointed translator,
Described assignments to him while the class watched.
The attention mortified me. My classmates' curiosity at
  sounds
Not theirs turned my speech into performance. Once,
  the teacher said "It's
Like music to my ears" in class, amidst bongos and
  maracas. After that, I
Gave translated instructions brusquely, furtively, the
  words
Kicking out of my mouth before others could hear. I
  wanted to
Hide the sounds. Instead, I was forced to sing my
  strangeness aloud.

John bore the brunt of my shame, and I am still sorriest
    to him,
Quizzed for a year on assignments relayed mostly
    through anger. Drinking
Xifan at home, my parents asked about my new role
    translating for "the
Zhang classmate," delighted I could make use of our
    language. I admit,
Chinese does chime like music. I couldn't have
    deadened my
Shifting tones in that classroom if I'd wanted. We
Rang words back and forth to each other like strings
    plucked on a
Zither. So what if our speaking sounds like singing. We
Curved our mouths around the four tones as children
    for a reason.
Syllables gallop from my open mouth and John
    understands them.
Yes, learning language is a kind of incantation.
    We chant pinyin down a poster.
We say *Ah* hoping someone will understand and
    answer.

Study in Blue

In French, duck-blue means green
gleam of a mallard. Blue applied to steak
means one layer rawer than bloody. French blue
is economical, multi-purpose as dish soap.

Speakers of languages without a word for blue
describe the sky as having no color. I asked Pierre
why blue means so many things. He said
We don't have that many words.

Lapis. Lapels. Irish
calla lilies. Herbal
vanilla. The pearled
caves of orchids.

The years my grandmother
begged us to speak
in her language. The color
of a sky full of tropical storm.
The halo around a fading
tattoo, a bowl used to crush
sesame seeds, a bruise.

It rhymes but isn't right.
Not blue, but the sound
blue makes. The last sound
in my grandmother's name.

While Peering in the Mirror

The underside of my tongue blushes purple.
Uprooted irises dry in the field.

Crows turn the furrow the way the farmer's
daughter tosses her hair. Human faces are easy

for corvids to remember. With enough
concentration, my eyes appear purple.

The nature of the world appears to be feathered.
The confetti bark of eucalyptus trees invites fire.

In Sydney, flammable trees form a cathedral.
In Milan, my mother brushes her cheeks

with holy water. I travel past old fields
I believe to be far from her. The lamp

leading us forward runs on animal fat and air.
Faraway, she fills a quiet theater with her laughter.

One Blue Sound

My greatest sin must be that I still dream

of disappearing. Any view of fields so green they glow

like an azure fur preened by the stirred

trail of tractors turns my thoughts to soybean plants

and foreign language. I cannot achieve incomprehensibility

without singing. In first grade I invented a secret

language to protect the contents of my diary.

In those pages of half-moons I confessed

my heart's panic for the first time. At the end

of her life, Didion's Maria dreams of canning.

Apricots and summer squash mute enough

to hold her desert heart without cracking.

If silence were a language one could learn

and wield in the heat of fieldwork.

The nearest thing: green promise

of distance between one blue sound

and the next word, spoken aloud

on my tongue and heard.

Missing You

Somewhere, a scallop is blinking
its two hundred blue eyes.
This isn't true. The airstrip lights
at O'Hare are steady blue dots
among droplets on the plane window.
They burn no matter the weather,
no matter what any animal wants.

青

Blue brick moves through
a green dream. Bluebells
in my beard. Fog in the mirror.
I dreamt a blue so green
I woke smelling eucalyptus.
A slim green can holds
vegetable ends. I peel apples
in the blue afternoon. The skin falls
in a perfect ring. I do not think
of my mother asleep. The jade
bracelet she gave me shattered
on a tennis court floor. The gift
of clarity is rare. Our bus climbs
air thinned to green. I wanted her
to forgive me without knowing I was blue.
I wanted to forgive her for knowing.

Hymn

I want to stop taking drugs
for granted. Desire makes me
serious. I keep busy by looking
for the center. Squirrel tail:
blue slivers cohere around a wire.
The burning between my back
and sternum. How we wake
in pairs. In Paris, I made
a nest in the idea of you.
You read aloud in a language
I could not understand. You made
sense without me. In the absence
of pure translation, pure sentences.
We cannot know. We shed our coats.
We measure the sun against
our watches, wanting seconds
back from the dark. I touch your cheek
to mark the picture in my head I make.
We fall asleep just long enough to dream
in private *fear, so thoroughly ours.*

The Road from the Mountains

I recently learned it is possible to peel sheep:
in one motion, like tearing a grapefruit skin. Clean.
The known easily becomes strange: Rough grass.
Animal body. Naked core. Like chewing through a peach

to find an almond in the center. At each exit, I imagine
strip mall delis with off-brand dairy, cheap butter,
soft cheese. The town snoozing through its sermons.
A flavor I have never tasted and can barely imagine

entering my body. How to hold on to the strange names?
What trash collects beneath ballpark bleachers.
How to arrive at the astonishing heart? We drive
through fields of prairie wool. After miles, the road goes flat.

We pass weigh stations, ignite Chevron signs
in our high-beams. We play Alicia Keys. Gas and singers
had different names once, like cities. I soar
when I taste them: Calso. Aguello. Strawberry.

IV

Before Desire

When we were pelicans we lived in the air
and the sea, dipping to catch fish

for each other. Flight was nothing special.
We cleaned our wings. Sometimes the catch

swam down and we dove with such force
that our bodies became blades through the water.

We did not hope for anything.
Our way of being in the world

was the only one we wanted. My feathers
moved well and precisely. I could not

sing. Each day my mouth held only what
I could eat. At night, the saltwater clung

to our chests like fur. We had no dreams.
When we were pelicans, we had no dreams.

Lake Lanier

After jumping into the water to retrieve
my little brother's lost sock and paddling back
to our rented boat to haul myself up, gleaming
with warm lake water so muddy it is tea-colored,
my big sister tells me a secret. *You know*
there are dead people at the bottom of this lake,
she says, as my body dries in the July sun,
because of the dam. I do not want to hear this,
do not want to picture a waterlogged
mother waiting for her children to return
from school at the narrow kitchen door,
pruney from the years, unclear whether her
frown lines are from water or worry.

It's so deep your heart could stop from the cold—
a force field around those houses and hearts,
shield to even the bravest diver. I look
around at the families on their squat boats
like ours. They buckle kids into life vests,
drink beer, slather sunscreen onto their white arms,
unaware. To them the lake is still a lake.
It is too late for me now, and though I am tired,
and eight, I think of the cold water around my feet
moments earlier, how it hurt my ankles, icy compared
to the sun-warmed surface. And I can't help
imagining, despite everything, diving headfirst
into the mud, swimming until the brown turns
black, so cold it tightens my chest, so deep

I might escape the surface world
for just a bit, kick down to the village
that can never tell me its secret
and sit with them for a minute
or two before I return, limbs tingling.

The Ocean in Miniature

By the time we reach the deep sea exhibit,
the bodies are so strange that they remind me
of nothing until I see the names:

*Cookie-cutter shark. Spaghetti worm.
Moon jelly.* What somersaulting tongues
hungrily christened this sea?

Of course marine worms look like pasta
heaped on the ocean floor. My favorites
are the *chicken liver sponge* and *bloodbelly jelly*.

I hold the names like ripe fruit in my mouth.
My mind turns easily to the seabed where hagfish
slide between whale ribs, ensuring no death is wasted.

What enables me to enter this dream
is not just the thrill of the unfamiliar—
although I love this, too. A bit like the vertigo

of watching snow and imagining myself
in a shaken globe, the sudden snap
of scale rendered legible. Here, the vastness

of a word like *depth* or *death* or *knowing*
becomes *bowl sponge. Comb jelly.*
Things that fit in my palm.

I want the world like this, suspended,
rendered by God or a scientist into something
made for my hands, my human tongue.

Leaving Lisbon

I watch fog coat the hills.
Every new place reminds me
of an old place. A field I saw
in a painting. Coastal California.
We pried mussels off the rocks
with gloved hands and rinsed them
in the sink. I remember the quiet
clicking their alive backs made
as they soaked.

The water in this air is old
and shared. I wanted out
of the cold known. I tied my mind
around a town. I arrived
and my longing doubled.
There must be a center to all this
wanting. Two shells close to protect
their emptiness. There must be something
older than the moon. The opposite of
there is nothing new under the sun.

Phenomenology Study /
Elegy for Island Love

The banana plant that thrashed outside my lover's window
seemed unreal. Our hours together felt like a dream:
how he nudged a spider up the shower tile
with a cupped hand, unwilling to hurt anything
alive. How unlike me, watching the slow turn
of the ceiling fan, wondering whose stanza I'd slipped
into. Once, I could see how badly he wanted me
to say something honest. My constellation of facts
could not parry his grief. *The tide is low / The limes
are ripe / I saw a cauliflower jellyfish today.* The sea
we shared, a surface I could not bear to speak past.
I used my words. I wove a net of truth and cast it
between us. And when it rained, I listened
to the banana leaves, believing I could hear their color.

Recurring Dream
of Escape

All at once I am small
beyond belief. I buy yogurt
at the supermarket.
Nothing else concerns me.
Those who know my name
are only visiting. Or, they work
the register and allow me
to remind them vaguely
of their daughters. On days
it does not rain, I swim
in the sea. I am, for once,
nothing, smaller than nothing,
beholden to no one, friendless,
unmeasured, unwitnessed,
and in this way finally free.

He Sleeps

I shared dark cherries with my brother
after a night walk on the beach. Perched on rocks,

we watched each wave turn the boulders sleek.
Thrilling, sitting so near dark water,

out of reach. In the dark, everything is a dream:
the faraway freighter silently blinking.

The patch of water shaped like a sea lion turning
its body back to the deep. Sometimes, I wonder

if memories are kinder than they seem.
The lover I could not touch turning easily

away in sleep. My mother tucking fruit
into the suitcase to prepare for my leaving.

The years my brother crouched in the dark garage,
building furniture, alone with her—always, my leaving.

The night I thought I'd lost him forever,
summer hummed, a low thrum. My phone buzzed

through dark heat. We reach into darkness
and come back empty. The night tide recedes.

Somewhere far from any water, he sleeps.

She Has Dreamt Again of Water

Of course in the story the exile is beautiful.
The moon: what better place, luminous,
feminine, impossibly distant? What better home

for the lonely body than another lonely,
celestial body? When I visited the moon, the lady
was sleeping. Her open palm twitched. Outside,

no wind stirred the pale sheets. They were dry;
I took them down. No rain. No rain forever—
I wonder what she misses most about Earth.

Sometimes, I wish I could be her—impossibly
distant, immortally distant, my escape
transformed into myth—I want people to look

at the pale crescent and think they see
the shape of me. I would dance, alone
and mesmerizing. When she wakes,

she does not weep. She has dreamt again
of water, that place where the river
meets the sea, where long-legged birds

tiptoe through the cordgrass, dipping
their heads to feed. The miracle of one body
emptying itself into another is the same miracle

of not being the only body. She looks around.
The sheets have been taken down.
I am long gone by then.

Returning to the Village

That gray hut is where I first learned to swim. They pushed us
through a gap in the floorboards. Dropped down a rope
to hold. It took us several panicked kicks to find

that we knew how to do it. Once under, our eyes adjusted
to the salt's burn and gleam. The fish did not care.
They turned their long bodies and became something's dinner.

At home, toweled off, we ate from plates of tasteless crackers
bought from the only supermarket with sides salt-faded
to white. The woman who owns it still lives inside.

She has no sons; the fish she sells comes frozen
in boxes from the mainland. I once saw her crouch
on the jetty at dawn and place a basket into the water,

raise it again full of leathery fish flopping against her arms.
She gutted them. They were so small. I watched
her toss what was left of them back to the ocean.

I Met My Loneliness

on the train back from the secondhand shop;
wearing a green rain jacket, he was watching
a video on his phone and laughing privately,
glancing up every few stops to check
that no one was looking. The spot next to him
was too small to sit in, so I remained
standing, in my used boots, holding a rain-
weakened paper bag of clothes. We got off
at the same stop. He took the exit I always do.
At the intersection, it began raining
in earnest, enough that I shielded my face
with my hands and ran, clomped along
unable to see, until I remembered to check
whether my loneliness was behind me,
turned, and saw only the street.

I Drive as My Family Sleeps

I take us south, toward home. The work is done,
the truck loaded and chugging. Even the rain
has stopped for a while. Earlier, my parents ate together
for the first time in years, holding foil-wrapped pork
on the edge of a cargo bed, their knees almost touching.

I wonder if we know how to be with each other
without labor. Even this journey north to clear out
an old warehouse by ourselves, the five of us
refusing to hire help, proves just how far we'll travel
for a meal together. Reunited, we wrap furniture.
We take out garbage, collect branches to toss
in the strip mall dumpster. Even the youngest of us,
my brother, understands what is required. He learns
to maneuver the truck in the rain and carries his best tools
from home. I glance in the rearview. For once,

everyone is asleep, necks slack, mouths gently opening.
Soon, we will arrive, unload the truck, lift dressers, scrub scales
from the fish for dinner, working again at our lives. But for now,
this quiet mile is the only thing on earth that is ours.

V

老家

At the airport my father balks
at the weight of my suitcase, the crushed wheel

that will not spin, the way I've had to drag
the bag over grime and carpet instead.

With one stoop he lifts the suitcase by its middle
onto his shoulder and walks.

I think of eggplants.
The tight rows he showed us

with so much pride, each green tuft
nurtured by a shoulder carrying water.

The joy when we found one
hidden in the shade like a peeled egg.

Winters on the farm, how he chewed
raw cloves of garlic, eyes smarting, to fill his belly.

His home a night's train ride from the nearest city:

the rough mud-brick walls with straw
sticking out, the hard beds, the well

with a metal lid for drinking water
where I once found a fish so tiny I mistook it for light.

The Question

Unfortunately, I want to fall in love. A breathy singer in my ear is listing colors like a prayer: *oh pink and blue*, oh green machine smoothie, oh gold status (premium), save us from distance-lust. In this Icarus airplane I skim the sky into fatless milk. The cream collects on my wings. The Atlantic froths with the wake of ships cargoing, cruising, bellying the water with metal. I am learning to be a better animal. When the chorus finally emerges from the strings, I am breathing. For the first time, I feel my body trying to teach me the meaning of the word *fertile*. *The first time* is a language I refuse to let go extinct. Though the milk sours hourly. Though this tundra in the sky keeps melting. Let me have the question. Let me have someone to teach the taste of ice cream.

The Magic of Eating Garbage

My mother taught me that being a trash can is hard
but worthwhile. She martyred herself against the scraps.

Pan scrapings went into porridge. She drank days-old
fish soup and beamed when the bowl was clean.

I've learned from her; I prepare meals
based on what most recently expired.

Stale chips with old hummus, stews of half-opened
spaghetti sauce, rice from yesterday's cooker.

Once, I ate a tub of Greek yogurt a week after it soured.
It makes no sense; I went out for a restaurant dinner after.

But I'm still surprised when guests reject
my best offers: salmon filet that's one day away

from the date! Milk on the verge of curdling!
To rescue mismatched wilting vegetables

into gumbo, stir fry, soup—I want to feed my guests
the magic of reuse. To take what we stop accounting for

and make it into stew—it's alchemy. The world
tasting, for once, abundant. Brand-new.

Bracing Myself Against Sea Wind Along the Coast You Call Home

Each time I smell the sea
I begin a new life. How many lives
have I spent loving you?

Migration

These days, I dream more and more of the sea
in November, monsoon season, swell
season far from here, free
from the close heat of home, where shells
stick to my toes. It is nowhere near
this life, this body, my mother,

which is where the dream began, mother
tells me. *You dreamed of flying over the sea,*
of leaving everything near
for something far, and I hear her swell
with pride, at this dream which is a shell
of a memory, at my early desire to be free

from known life. Grades. Groceries. Free
samples of cookies. Wings big enough for my mother
to be carried. She shows me the shell-
shaped scar from her trip with my father to the sea,
when they biked even though she was swelled
with my brother, and she fell, and the gear pierced near

her knee, the cut, the gush, the near-
est hospital too far away and not free.
Before the body can heal it must swell,
and hers did, the skin blooming before a mother-
of-pearl scar closed it neatly. Her sea-
son of letting things run freely. Now, shell-

ing snow peas, she urges me to stay, where there is shel-
ter, a bright future, and family near
to me. She wants to know why I long for the sea.
I wish I could say what I need to be free

from, what thing. Not any particular, even my mother.
In the summer, both places swell

with heat. It is more than giving up one swel-
tering season for another. There is a place where red-shelled
crabs migrate together, at new moon the mothers
dancing in the water, claws upraised, near
each other, to shake their eggs free.
A yearly survival pilgrimage to the sea.

One day, I will show my mother the swells,
how the sea collapses, collects itself into shell
-shaped waves, the way they pull you near before letting you free.

Today Is

the kind of day that makes me want to cook
a pancake breakfast for all of my friends.

Spent it mostly barefoot on sand
and driftwood floors. Someone won an award.

Someone had the same stress dream as me;
we woke to a blue sky and the sea

a Mediterranean calm. The anonymous yachts
bobbing in the cove could belong to anyone.

Sophie taught me the phrase *cave kiss*
for when a droplet falls on your head.

I used the phrase *lime eyes* to describe
how keenly Abby spots the shiny prize,

green nestled among green, teetering high
on a dry-season branch for our rake to wrestle free.

A gift of chili paste from Anom is waiting for the fish.
I count the joys around me like rooms, incredulous.

The rind of foraged lime I slide into the fish's sliced gut;
the blaze of Tom's torch illuminating the cave's clear pool;

Toby's bare soles crossing the sandy plain of the deck;
saltwater evaporating off the shoulders of Damo and Lex.

I want a map of this, a floorplan of gratitude
at last, without fear. I want to know

it is mine enough to live in. It is here.

Motherhood in the Climate Crisis

means my womb is a bomb I choose
to wield. Violence precipitates peace,
according to every revolution.
After acid precipitation fells
each chestnut tree, I will teach
my daughter extinct species
from old paintings. The rind-filled
melons of still lifes lying sliced open
next to a skull. The wrinkle-faced dogs
we bred until they couldn't breathe.

I need to believe she will grow old
so I can teach her my secrets: how to fix
her eye on the distant sea to watch
for coming wind. How to wind
her arms up for a perfect cartwheel.
How to give an animal a proper burial.
How to find where life still runs rampant:
Dandelion roots. Wild onions. How to name
what we've lost when she bites into the harvest.

Sea Swim

The ocean is a wedding waiting room.
Quiet and separate from the visible world,
she glows a filtered-through gold.
Here, every dream is still possible.
The miracle of vertical flight is easy
as a raised foot or wing. I glide down
though my body is already rising up.

I told Tina I came to the island
because I fell in love twice.
This is still the shortest true explanation.
Inevitable, the kiss that waits at the end
of the sea's long room. Still, I hold.
I rise. I do everything I can to stay.

CODA

大连 / Dalian

I touched the sea in the city where my grandparents met.

The day was blue, the water rough and green.

It was October, the ocean finally open for harvest.

I practiced the word for *abalone* in my mind.

鲍鱼, 鲍鱼. A fish in a fish, a fish in a word, a fish in a pocket of light.

My grandparents' street must have been a pocket of light when they met.

No one knew until the two young neighbors' love had already taken hold.

Time took my grandfather young. Everyone agrees.

My grandmother, alive and ninety, holds on alone.

This is the same city where I learned to speak and walk. I left young, before memory could take hold.

No one told my mother her father had died, because she was pregnant with me.

Perhaps he held part of his world by the coast open after he left.

鲍鱼, 鲍鱼. The word for *hold* and the word for *fish*.

Friends ask how I can love the sea if I grew up hours inland from the coast.

I never knew. For years I held this place only as an idea.

Here at last, I edge my sneakers away from oncoming waves. I splash the surface of the seawater with my palms.

When my mother found out her father was gone, she said I quaked in her belly so hard she thought she would split open.

When I arrive, the abalone we will eat are already split and shining.

My whole life, arriving at any sea, I have reached for the water with my hands.

Notes

"IF WORDS COST NOTHING"

Seven named zones defined by sun: This phrase refers to both horizontal oceanic zones, which are defined by their distance from shore (intertidal, neritic, and oceanic), and vertical oceanic zones, which are defined by their access to sunlight (epipelagic, mesopelagic, bathypelagic, abyssopelagic, and hadalpelagic). "Defined by sun" refers to the vertical, or photic, zones. This poem takes the liberty of counting the third horizontal oceanic zone as a repeat of all five vertical photic zones, bringing the total zone count to seven.

I
———————————————————————————

"LEARNING MONEY IN REVERSE"

姥姥 (lǎo lao) means "maternal grandmother."

"WHAT DO CORAL EVEN GET STRESSED ABOUT"

Current events: The title and first line of this poem quote a Tumblr exchange between users dcksp8jr and one-hamburger, which has since been immortalized as the meme "Coral stress."

Coral takes one look / at the police officer on trial and bleaches: I wrote this poem in the summer of 2021, around the time of the sentencing hearing for Derek Chauvin, the former Minnesota police officer who was tried and convicted for murdering George Floyd.

"I CROSSED THE SEA BOARDWALK"

Aristotle thought they come from nothing: In *The Book of Eels*

(*Ålevangeliet*), Patrik Svensson describes Aristotle's response to the mystery of eel reproduction. Aristotle considers an evaporated pond with a hardened bottom and observes that, with the first rain, "suddenly, the pond is once more full of eels. Suddenly, they're just there. The rainwater brings them into existence."

II

"MIDDEN / APPETITE"

In a California midden / where Chinese orchard workers lived: This poem references the Arboretum Chinese Labor Quarters site, an archaeological site in the Stanford University Arboretum where Chinese employees maintaining orchards, vineyards, wineries, and iconic Stanford landscape features lived from 1883 to 1925.

"HUMMINGBIRDS"

the trucks / that transferred a thousand sick prisoners / into the cells of the well. Five men died today: In May 2020, prisoners infected with COVID-19 were transferred from the California Institution for Men in Chino to San Quentin State Prison, which had previously had no COVID-19 cases. The transfer caused an outbreak that a state judge cited as "the worst epidemiological disaster in California correctional history."

"HILTON HEAD"

The format of this poem, and in particular the first words in each sentence, takes inspiration from Sophie Klahr's poem "Vetiver."

"BY THESE THINGS WE LIVE"

to comprehend it back: This line responds to the last line of "My God, It's Full of Stars" by Tracy K. Smith: "So brutal and alive it seemed to comprehend us back."

Bach's last piece, / unfinished, spells his name in the notes: Johann Sebastian Bach's final contrapunctus, "The Art of Fugue," spells out his surname B-A-C-H as a musical motif through the sequence B♭ - A - C - B♮. In German, B♮ is called H.

The other golden record sounds: Three of Bach's pieces are included on the Voyager Golden Record, a phonograph record launched aboard both the Voyager 1 and Voyager 2 in 1977. This is more pieces than any other artist represented on the record.

III

"ENDEAVOUR"

a sequined dinosaur rotates, midair: Several images in this poem reference the documentary *Return to Space* (2022).

先蹦一蹦，在看: This phrase (xiān bèng yī bèng, zài kàn!) roughly means "Let's jump around a little first, then see!"

"ABECEDARIAN FOR PINYIN"

Ü *which sounds like the word for fish*: The vowel Ü is pronounced like 鱼 (yú) which means "fish."

"兰"

兰 (lán) commonly refers to orchids (i.e. 兰花). It is also used in phrases that describe lilies, magnolia, and floral fragrances. It rhymes with the character 蓝 (lán), which means "blue."

"ONE BLUE SOUND"

Didion's Maria dreams of canning: This line references the protagonist of Joan Didion's *Play It as It Lays*, Maria Wyeth.

"青"

青 (qīng) describes a color somewhere between blue and green. It can also mean "clear."

"HYMN"

fear, so thoroughly ours: This line quotes Addendum III of Henri

Michaux's *Miserable Miracle*. Michaux, in describing a psychedelic feeling of non-duality, says, "The hymn is the most natural form for this, next to which our Christian liturgies with their fear, so thoroughly ours, of not contradicting themselves, pale in comparison" (p. 176).

IV

"BEFORE DESIRE"

When we were pelicans: This line takes inspiration from the opening couplet of Aracelis Girmay's poem "Science": "We were trying to refind the eye & brain / we had when we were pelicans."

"THE OCEAN IN MINIATURE"

By the time we reach the deep sea exhibit: The species names in this poem come from the marine dioramas in the Hall of Ocean Life at the American Museum of Natural History in New York City.

"SHE HAS DREAMT AGAIN OF WATER"

When I visited the moon, the lady / was sleeping: "The lady" throughout this poem is Chang E, a goddess from Chinese mythology who (in some versions) flew to the moon after swallowing an elixir of immortality.

V

"老家"

老家 (lǎo jiā) means "hometown" or "ancestral home."

"THE QUESTION"

oh pink and blue: This line quotes the song "Pink & Blue" by Tycho.

Coda

"大连 / DALIAN"

大连 (dà lián) is a coastal town in northeastern China.

鲍鱼 (bào yú) means "abalone." The components of the leftmost word, 鲍, separate into the word for "fish" (鱼) and the root of the word for "hold" (抱).

Acknowledgments

No book is a lonely endeavor, and I am grateful for the people, places, organizations, and systems that allowed this collection to mature.

Parts of this collection were written and revised on the ancestral lands of the Muwekma Ohlone, Lenape, Muscogee Creek, Cherokee, Gadigal, and Dharug people. Parts of this collection were also inspired by or written on Christmas Island, a place made habitable by the enslaved labor of Cocos Malay people and the indentured labor of Chinese and Malay people, including women from the Samsui District of Canton Province, from the late nineteenth to mid-twentieth century. I write in the shade of trees planted by others long before.

This manuscript would not exist without the kindness of Anak Pulau and Islanders who welcomed me into their homes, shared their knowledge, and allowed Christmas Island to truly become part of my life. Thanks especially to Chris Su, Hafiz Masli, Oliver Lines, Jason Turl, Tanya Detto, and Craig Wood.

My trips to Christmas Island were generously supported by a William W. and Janet F. Crandall Beagle II Award for independent research from Stanford University and a Fulbright scholarship through the Shire of Christmas Island and Western Sydney University. I am grateful for the material support and spiritual validation that these grants provided, in addition to valuable time on Christmas Island.

In kindergarten, I wanted to be an author when I grew up. I extend my biggest gratitude to K–12 teachers but especially to Kathy Howard, Marcia Follensbee, Mary Rowlett, Rebecca Johnson, Scott McCord, Roberta Manheim, and Tim Church, who encouraged me toward this dream and nurtured the creative writing spark in me before I fully knew its form. Mrs. Follensbee, one day I'll find a way to include "akimbo" in one of my books.

To my poetry teachers: Esther Lin, Solmaz Sharif, Kai Carlson-Wee, and Louise Glück, for teaching me how to read well, revise myself, and become a better poet. Louise, I wish I could have said goodbye. Thank you for all that you taught me.

I am grateful to the editors of the following journals who first gave many of these poems a home:

Bear Review: "I Crossed the Sea Boardwalk";
Breakwater Review: "Garbage Boogie";
Copper Nickel: "Learning Money in Reverse";
Ecotone: "Information Worker at the End of the World";
ENTROPY: "Before Desire";
Epiphany Magazine: "He Sleeps," "The Magic of Eating Garbage," and "The Ocean in Miniature";
Georgia Review: "Hummingbirds," "I Drive as My Family Sleeps," "Lake Lanier," and "The Road from the Mountains";
Gulf Coast: "大连 / Dalian";
Hopkins Review: "The World's Heart";
Inverted Syntax: "By These Things We Live";
Missouri Review: "If Words Cost Nothing," "Motherhood in the Climate Crisis," "One Blue Sound," and "The Question";
Not Very Quiet: "老家" (originally published as "Hometown");
Passengers Journal: "Study in Blue," "兰," and "青";
Philadelphia Stories: "Abecedarian for Pinyin";
Plainsongs: "Returning to the Village";
Portland Review: "Midden / Appetite";
Quarterly West: "Hymn" and "Sonnet of Tropical Excess";
Radar Poetry: "Keeping House";

Raleigh Review: "While Peering in the Mirror";
Sho: "Leaving Lisbon";
The Common: "Phenomenology Study / Elegy for Island Love";
The Offing: "Endeavour"; and
Under a Warm Green Linden: "What do coral even get stressed about?"

Thanks especially to the editors at *Bear Review* for nominating "I Crossed the Sea Boardwalk" as a finalist for the 2024 Michelle Boisseau Prize; to the editors at *Philadelphia Stories* and Cynthia Arrieu-King for selecting "Abecedarian for Pinyin" as runner-up for the 2022 Sandy Crimmins Poetry Contest; to the editors of *Breakwater Review* for nominating "Garbage Boogie" as a finalist for the 2021 Peseroff Prize; and to the editors of *Inverted Syntax* and Khadijah Queen for selecting "By These Things We Live" as a runner-up for the 2020 Sublingua Prize.

I am grateful for the editorial insight and patience of Claire Bowman, Esther Lin, Soham Patel, Chaelee Dalton, Christian Thorsberg, and Dawn Angelica; thank you for your generous attention to my work.

Some of the poems in this collection first appeared in the chapbooks *She Has Dreamt Again of Water* (Diode Editions, 2022) and *Survived By: An Atlas of Disappearance* (Host Publications, 2024). I have eternal gratitude for Patty Paine and Zoe Shankle Donald at Diode Editions and Annar Veröld and Claire Bowman at Host Publications for believing in my work early on. Your love for poetry and dedication to the chapbook form gave me a first taste of how publishing can connect people and how a slim volume can give an emerging writer hope.

I'm deeply grateful to the jurors who read my work and believed in it. To Major Jackson for selecting my work for the inaugural Vanderbilt Literary Prize; thank you. This is a life-changing honor.

Gratitude to the team at Vanderbilt University Press for bringing this book to fruition, particularly Patrick Samuel for his unflagging support.

Thank you to Noelle Falcis Math for being my champion and guide through this transition into a new relationship with my writing.

Thanks to the friends who provided comfort and guidance at various points in this book's journey: Juliana Chang, Jeff Adler, Will Maxen, Sarah Wilson, Glyn Hunt, Daniel Uncapher, and mick powell.

To Justin, for tolerating all my book-related decisions and for consistently terrible title suggestions.

To Catherine, my eternal confidant and co-thinker.

To the beloveds whose care has buoyed me through verse and much more.

And to my family, without whom I haven't much love to write of at all.